WILD HORSE ANNIE

Friend OF THE Mustangs

WILD HORSE ANNIE

Friend OF THE Mustangs

TRACEY FERN ★ Pictures by STEVEN SALERNO

Farrar Straus Giroux • New York

Annie had loved horses for as long as she could remember, especially the wild ones— mustangs!

When she was **just a speck of a girl**, she would sit on the rail of the corral at her family's ranch in Nevada, watching her pa tame the mustangs that he had captured from the great herds that galloped across the desert.

Annie learned to ride tucked up tight in front of Pa on the back of his trusty tamed mustang, Old Baldy. When Pa clucked his tongue, Annie would clutch Old Baldy's bristly mane to stay on as the horse galloped through the scrub. Soon she was riding alone through the sand and sagebrush that stretched from their ranch to the Sierra Nevada mountains. She even learned to gentle wild mustangs herself, using nothing more than a rope and her voice.

But in 1923, when Annie was eleven years old, she caught polio.

For a long time, she couldn't ride at all. She couldn't even walk. Annie was in a cast from her head to her hips. Day after day, in a hospital far from home, she stared at a painting of mustangs that hung in the hall outside her room. Annie liked to pretend she was winging along with that herd, fast and free and easy.

When Annie left the hospital, her spine was bent and her face was twisted. Everything ached all the time. Part of Annie just wanted to hide inside her house.

Instead, she got on a horse.

Annie said that horses took the pain away, at least for a little while. She never wanted to be without them.

Annie dreamed about finding someone who loved her, despite her bends and twists. Of course, that someone had to love horses, too, "only slightly less than he loves me," Annie joked. She found that someone in 1936, when she met Charlie.

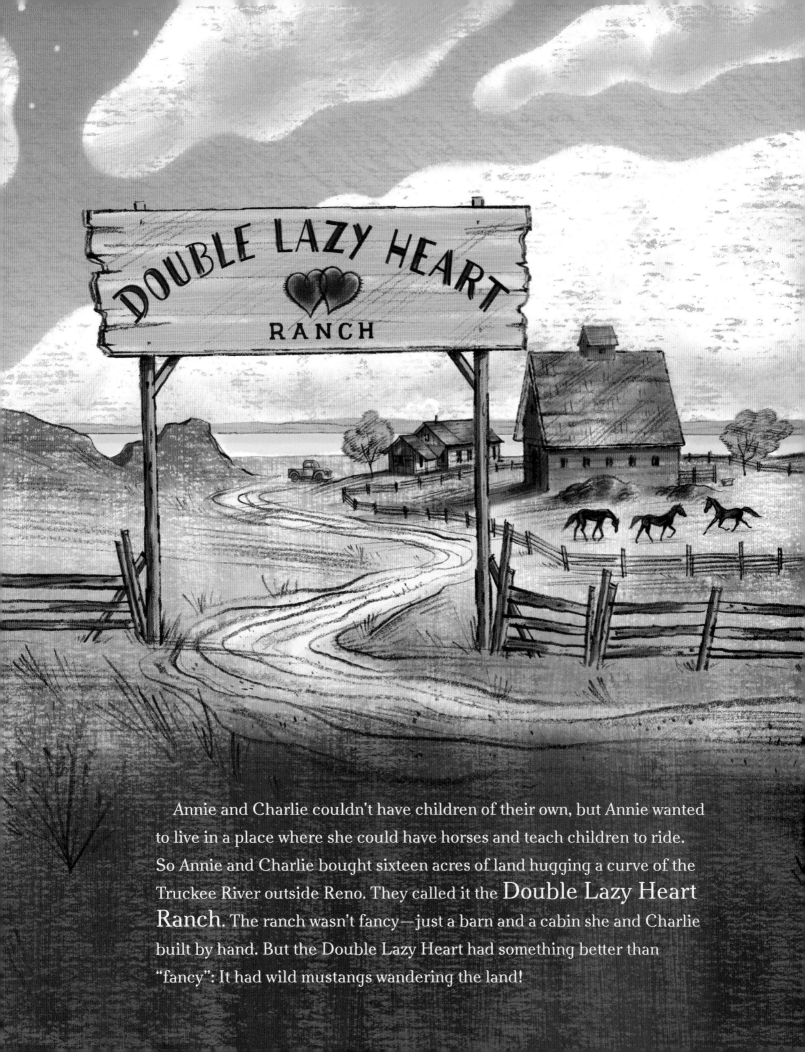

Annie and Charlie couldn't have children of their own, but Annie wanted to live in a place where she could have horses and teach children to ride. So Annie and Charlie bought sixteen acres of land hugging a curve of the Truckee River outside Reno. They called it the Double Lazy Heart Ranch. The ranch wasn't fancy—just a barn and a cabin she and Charlie built by hand. But the Double Lazy Heart had something better than "fancy": It had wild mustangs wandering the land!

By now, the great herds of Annie's childhood were gone—killed off by ranchers protecting their cattle's grazing land and hunters who sold them to slaughterhouses for use as pet food and fertilizer. But sometimes, in the quiet of morning, when the first squint of light pushed across the sky, Annie and Charlie caught a glimpse of a few mustangs that had come down from the foothills to drink from the river. They would stand on the rocks along the riverbank, still as sentinels, then wheel and be off.

Annie knew the mustangs weren't beautiful. Most were underfed, scruffy-looking critters, bony and squat. They were a patchwork of colors and patterns, and they had a patchwork history, too: The mustangs' ancestors were domesticated horses that had arrived with early explorers and settlers who came to live in the West. Through the years, those horses had escaped from their owners and turned wild.

But no matter their looks or their backgrounds, Annie thought mustangs were pure magic. She called them her "wild ones"— high-spirited, freedom-loving, and tough as barbed wire.

And, oh, those **mustangs** moved like they had wings, their hooves hardly touching the ground! Annie still dreamed of moving like that, **flying along with the herd.**

Then one morning in 1950, as Annie was driving along a twisting gravel road, she noticed a livestock truck packed with horses. Something about the animals just didn't look right, so she followed it to its destination—a slaughterhouse. When Annie peered into the back of the truck, she saw mustangs packed tight together, all of them injured.

"Where did these horses come from, and why are they in such terrible condition?" Annie asked the driver.

He told Annie that an airplane had swooped low over the desert while men aboard fired shotguns, chasing the mustangs into a makeshift corral. Some of the horses had been shot or trampled during the roundup. Soon, they were all going to be killed.

Annie had heard about these roundups before, but she hadn't really thought about them. Now, she couldn't stop.

Annie told Charlie what she had seen.

"So what are we going to do now?" Charlie asked.

Annie smiled. "We" was one of her favorite words. She figured that together, she and Charlie could do most anything.

The very next weekend, Annie and Charlie rode their horses, Hobo and Ranger, out into the desert and found the makeshift corral. In it were sixty mustangs, fearful and sweating. Oh, they were pitiful looking, without a blade of grass to eat or a drop of water to drink!

Annie and Charlie swung the gate wide. Those mustangs were gone in a thunder of hooves and a surge of dust . . . and so were Annie and Charlie!

But saving a few mustangs wasn't enough. Annie set up headquarters
at her kitchen table. She clickety-clacked away on her typewriter, sending
hundreds of letters to newspapers and politicians and neighbors and friends,
telling them about the roundups and asking for help in stopping them.
Charlie was her chief envelope stuffer.

Soon Annie started getting threats.

"You'd better lay off, sister," one person warned her. Another threatened
to hang her from a tree. Some folks thought there were too many mustangs
grazing on the public range. They said the horses were nothing but varmints
eating grass that their cattle needed. Other folks wanted to keep making a
profit by selling mustangs for slaughter. They all wanted Annie to hush up.

Instead, Annie spoke up louder.

Annie said talking in front of an audience made her feel like a "cat on a hot frying pan." She always worried over what people might think about the bends and twists she had from polio. But in 1952, Annie learned there was going to be a public meeting in the neighboring county about whether the government should allow another mustang roundup. She had to go.

When Annie and Charlie got to the meeting, Charlie crooned a few lines to make her feel better: *"He was just a lonely cowboy, with a heart so brave and true . . ."*

Annie knew she needed her heart to be brave and true, as well. She took a deep breath to stop her knees from shaking. Then she started telling folks about the mustang roundups.

"These horses are on public land, which makes them public property," Annie argued. She said that the mustangs that live on land owned by the state or federal government "belong to all Americans, to you and to me." And she insisted that mustangs on public land should be left alone.

Some folks tried to shout Annie down. But other folks listened.

Within a week, Annie's speech had helped convince the officials of that county to ban airplane roundups of wild horses on state-owned land. That was a start, but Annie knew the rustlers who were killing mustangs could just move to another county to hunt where there was no law against roundups.

Annie kept typing letters. She kept speaking out, too. Sometimes, Annie was in so much pain from her twisted spine that she felt like she was held together only by "a tight girdle and a case of hair spray." But she held together well enough to eventually speak in front of the Nevada Senate in 1955 about a bill to protect mustangs.

Annie entered the packed room in a crisp dress, high heels, and proper white gloves.

"Well, if it isn't Wild Horse Annie," one local rancher yelled. He didn't mean it kindly.

But Annie turned the joke around and asked everybody to call her Wild Horse Annie. The nickname spread like wildfire; soon it seemed like everyone knew about Wild Horse Annie and her mustangs.

THE NEVADA GAZETTE

10¢

WILD HORSE ANNIE: A Voice For Mustangs

THE NEVADA GAZETTE

ANNIE: A Voice For Mus

Annie's speech at that Senate meeting helped to convince the state of Nevada to ban the use of airplanes and other vehicles to capture wild horses on property owned by private citizens.

This statewide ban was better than nothing, but Annie still wasn't happy. Most land in Nevada wasn't private property; it was public property owned by the state or federal government. Her mustangs needed a law to protect them on public land throughout the state, not just in one county. But how would Annie get that law passed when ranchers and other powerful groups were fighting so hard against it?

Annie thought about her favorite word: "we." It was a little word, but it stood for something big—bigger than even her and Charlie. That gave Annie an idea.

"The children!" Annie told Charlie. Annie thought about all the children who had come to the Double Lazy Heart to learn how to ride. Whenever Annie had spoken about mustangs, the children had been eager to listen. Annie decided children would be her secret weapon to save the horses.

Annie got back to work at the kitchen table. She sent letters to schools all across the country, telling the children about the plight of the mustangs and asking them to help by writing their own letters and petitions to politicians in Washington, D.C.

One child wrote to Annie: "Today I read your news bulletin about the wild horses. When I saw those pictures, I started crying . . . Please, Annie, I'm only eleven, but I want to help."

And the children did help. From coast to coast, they joined Annie's "pencil brigade."

"Imagine—making DOG FOOD out of horses! We feed the birds, the squirrels, and the chipmunks to SAVE them! Let's see what we can do about saving the beautiful wild HORSES!!!!!!" some children wrote in a petition.

The letters to politicians grew from a trickle into a river and then into an all-out flood! Children sent thousands and thousands of letters to Washington.

"Am I going to be influenced by a bunch of children?" one politician finally wrote. "You bet your cowboy boots I am!"

In 1959, Congress passed a federal law that banned the use of planes and vehicles to round up mustangs on public land in all states. Folks called it the **Wild Horse Annie Law**.

The law was important, but Annie knew mustangs were still being slaughtered. They could still be rounded up and killed without using vehicles, and some people who wanted to kill the mustangs and some who were supposed to enforce the law just ignored it.

So Annie kept fighting for years, even after Charlie died, to have a broader law passed to protect the mustangs.

Most people thought Annie's dream of saving the wild horses would be impossible to achieve.

"I don't think the children would like it if I quit now," she said.

Finally, Annie called on her pencil brigade again.

Once more, children from across the country wrote letters. They held bake sales and car washes and sold bumper stickers and buttons to raise money to help the mustangs.

Annie went to visit the U.S. Congress in Washington, D.C. She brought wheelbarrows full of letters from children. She brought a class of sixth graders along to boost her courage, too. Then, she stood up to speak.

"Today," Annie said, "I am here to save a memory . . . Wild horses . . . are part of our national heritage, belonging to all the people of America."

Annie explained that the mustangs had helped to settle the wilderness, enforce law and order, bring civilization to a young country, and carry the mail over two thousand miles as part of the Pony Express, but they were still being "relentlessly and ruthlessly hunted" because enforcement of laws passed to protect them was "lukewarm to nonexistent."

Then Annie asked Congress to better protect the mustangs as "a gift to future generations."

WE LOVE
WILD HORSES
AND
BURROS

It did. In 1971, the U.S. Congress passed a broader law protecting wild horses and burros from being captured, killed, or disturbed in any way on public land. Annie promised that if mustangs were endangered again, "the fight will go on." She said that the mustang represented "freedom, pride, independence, endurance, and the ability to survive against unbelievable odds."

Just like Annie.

AUTHOR'S NOTE

I first learned about Wild Horse Annie in 1969, when I was a student in Mrs. Babbitt's first-grade class in Centerville, Massachusetts. I was one of the thousands of children who joined Wild Horse Annie's pencil brigade, writing letters to my legislators asking them to support the protection of mustangs. I never forgot the lesson of civic engagement that I learned from Wild Horse Annie.

Wild Horse Annie's real name was Velma Bronn Johnston. She was born near Reno, Nevada, on March 5, 1912. According to some estimates, there were two million mustangs roaming the American West at that time. Wild horses are not a native species in North America. Instead, the mustangs are descended from domesticated horses that escaped or were turned loose on the range. Some mustangs may even be the descendants of horses brought from Europe by Spanish conquistadores more than five hundred years ago. By the late 1600s, Plains Indians were capturing and taming mustangs, revolutionizing their cultures. White explorers and settlers tamed mustangs, too. Later residents also killed them. Hundreds of thousands of mustangs were rounded up all over the West and shipped off to wars or slaughterhouses, or shot for sport. By 1970, there were only about sixteen thousand wild horses left.

Velma and her pencil brigade worked tirelessly to change that. At a time when most women were expected to stay at home, Velma not only worked outside the home as an executive secretary at a bank, but also organized the sometimes-dangerous campaign to protect mustangs. After her husband, Charlie, died in 1964, Velma did most of this organizing single-handedly. It took her more than twenty years of hard work before the Wild Free-Roaming Horses and Burros Act became law in 1971. That law declared wild horses "living symbols of the historic and pioneer spirit of the West" and made it a crime to kill wild horses on most federal land.

Velma cherished the pen that President Eisenhower used to sign her bill into law. "If you look at it closely . . . you will see that . . . it is made of stardust and dreams come true . . . It is glowing with the red, white, and blue that is America, . . . containing the warmth and humanness and courage of its people," she wrote to a friend.

Today, just as in Wild Horse Annie's day, the question of what to do with America's wild horses is controversial. The 1971 law that Annie worked so hard to help enact has been amended several times. A federal agency called the Bureau of Land Management oversees the mustangs that live on public land in ten western states. The mustangs need to share this public land with other wild animals and with people who want to use the land for oil and gas extraction, mining, recreation, and livestock grazing. To control the mustang population, the Bureau now rounds up horses from the wild and holds them in pens or puts them up for sale or adoption. There are now more mustangs living in captivity than in the wild. Although the future of America's mustangs is uncertain, we are able to debate that future only because Wild Horse Annie looked into the back of a livestock truck one day and vowed to fight for our mustangs.

SELECTED SOURCES

Brungardt, Kurt. "Galloping Scared." *Vanity Fair*, Nov. 2006: 224.

Cruise, David, and Alison Griffiths. *Wild Horse Annie and the Last of the Mustangs.* New York: Scribner, 2010.

International Society for the Protection of Mustangs and Burros. ispmb.org.

Kania, Alan J. *Wild Horse Annie: Velma Johnston and Her Fight to Save the Mustang.* Reno: University of Nevada Press, 2012.

Morin, Paula. *Honest Horses: Wild Horses in the Great Basin*. Reno: University of Nevada Press, 2006.

Nebraska ETV Network and South Dakota Public Television. *Wild Horses: An American Romance*. netnebraska.org/basic-page/television/wild-horses-american-romance.

Ryden, Hope. *America's Last Wild Horses.* New York: Lyons Press, 1999.

"Statement of Mrs. Velma B. Johnston," *Hearings Before the Subcommittee on Public Lands of the Committee on Interior and Insular Affairs, House of Representatives, 92nd Congress, 1st Session, on H.R. 795, H.R. 5375, and Related Bills*, April 19–20, 1971: 78.

Stillman, Deanne. *Mustang: The Saga of the Wild Horse in the American West.* Boston: Houghton Mifflin, 2008.

Weiskopf, Herman. "Wild West Showdown: A Determined Lady Called Wild Horse Annie and Her Gang of School Kids Have Valiantly Risen to the Defense of the Beleaguered Mustang." *Sports Illustrated*, May 5, 1975: 82.

For Doug —T. F.

*For my grandfather Leon,
who loved his horses* —S. S.

Farrar Straus Giroux Books for Young Readers
An imprint of Macmillan Publishing Group, LLC
175 Fifth Avenue, New York, NY 10010

Text copyright © 2019 by Tracey Fern
Pictures copyright © 2019 by Steven Salerno
All rights reserved
Color separations by Embassy Graphics
Printed in China by Toppan Leefung Printing Ltd.,
Dongguan City, Guangdong Province
Designed by Roberta Pressel
First edition, 2019
1 3 5 7 9 10 8 6 4 2

mackids.com

Library of Congress Control Number: 2018944918
ISBN: 978-0-374-30306-8

Our books may be purchased in bulk for promotional, educational, or business use.
Please contact your local bookseller or the Macmillan Corporate and Premium Sales Department
at (800) 221-7945 ext. 5442 or by e-mail at MacmillanSpecialMarkets@macmillan.com.